# Sleep Training for the Exhausted Mom

A quick reference guide to sleep training and schedules for any age – from a mom's perspective

Christy L. Brunton

Special thanks to Owen Sears who designed the cover and
to Jenn Jacome for editing the book.

Grateful acknowledgment is made to Marc Weissbluth,
M.D. for permission to reprint excerpts of his writings.

ISBN-13: 978-1503191037
ISBN-10: 1503191036

Dedicated to my husband Troy
and my three beautiful girls,
Taylor, Kennedy and Reese

# Table of Contents

# Preface

I guess I should start with who I am and why I feel qualified to give you advice on babies and schedules. Let me take you back to spring 2005 when I was in the last trimester of my pregnancy with identical twin girls and was ordered to bed rest by my obstetrician. Not having much to do, I started reading books about what I should do when the babies finally arrive. I soaked up as much knowledge as I could by reading books on feeding and sleeping and what to do, what not to do. I thought I was completely ready for the journey that lied ahead.

Fast forward to May 16, 2005 when I became the proud mommy to two beautiful baby girls. We spent our first nine days in the neonatal intensive care unit (NICU) and I was given the green light to take them home on day ten. They were finally home. I was ready to start using all the knowledge I had learned in all these books…the problem was, I really couldn't remember any of it because at the time I read it, I wasn't putting it into action so it just didn't stick.

I assume if you are reading this book now you are just like I was in those first few weeks. You are at a new level of exhaustion that is hard to explain to anyone. You are trying to be the best hostess to all those people who want to drop by to say hi. You want to keep a semi-clean house so people won't think you are totally out of it. And, you are just trying to get all the feeding and sleeping stuff to work together so you can fit in a twenty minute nap. Am I speaking your language yet?

That's where I come in.

Let me give you a bit more background. The spoiler alert is I did make it through all of those things and now have two nine-year olds who are now in fourth grade (let me tell you, third grade and fourth grade are difficult but that is a different book for another time) and a six-year old daughter who is in first grade. When my twins were six weeks old, I joined my local twins club and I can still remember sitting next to a red-headed mom who had twin boys and looked all put together and I remember grilling her before and after the meeting and many meetings to come about "How do I get the girls to sleep…and more importantly, when do they sleep through the night?" I honestly don't remember her advice (I was a little tired those days), but I do know at some point someone, maybe it was her, pointed me in the direction of a few sleep books which I somehow found the time to read.

Two years later, I found myself as vice-president and then president of the twins club for several years and it was amazing how many women I met during that time. My girls were two at the time and the days of worrying about them sleeping through the night were long gone. I had new twin challenges to ponder (again, a topic for another book I will find time to write one day). The common thread between all of the moms I met during the nearly nine years I have been involved with the twins club so far, is every single one of them would come to a meeting with one mission in mind...I need help and, specifically, I want you to tell me how I can get my babies to sleep. Oh, please just tell me how I can get them to sleep. And, when will they sleep through the night?

And so, as I did every time, I would promise them this stage is temporary and they would make it through this stage and next month there would be a new worry. Then, I would tell them about sleep training and my tips and tricks to get babies sleeping. Low and behold, at the next few meetings, these same moms would pop back in and be amazed the advice was working.

After I got the same question so many times, I decided it was time to put my advice in writing and when my fellow moms of multiples would ask the popular sleep question, I would just shoot them over my advice in email which then turned into what is now known as "Christy's famous sleep training cliff notes." The goal of these notes is for you to have a quick reference guide to get you started and something you can turn to often as your baby grows.

It gives you the highlights of a book called "Healthy Sleep Habits, Happy Child" by Marc Weissbluth, M.D. which became my baby bible for my twin's first three years of life and then again when I had my third child. I would recommend you reading his book in its entirety but I know the reality is you are just too tired right now to do that, so use these notes now to get you started and turn to Dr. Weissbluth's book for more in-depth learning. This quick reference guide should give you just enough of the good stuff to develop a plan you can implement right away and get everyone (including yourself) sleeping again.

And one more thing, I understand my children are now older and a lot has changed in the past six years, but I do know this topic is something that stays consistent. I popped into a twins club meeting recently to say hi and wasn't surprised to hear the same exact conversations going on and questions being asked that I had witnessed years earlier and asked myself ten years ago. Teaching your children good sleep habits early on is something that will stay with them their entire lives.

And, if you still don't believe me, ask my friend Lauren who has sextuplets. I gave her the notes and she was able to apply them to not one, but six babies and was able to get them on a consistent schedule including naps and sleeping through the night. I am not going to say it is easy. It takes patience, dedication and, most importantly, consistency. But, if you are willing to dedicate a few weeks to it, the rewards will take you all the way into their school-age years.

Good luck and get some sleep!

# Foreword

When I was pregnant with my sextuplets, I sought advice from other moms of multiples. How in the world was I going to handle six babies?! The answer I got over and over again: get them on a schedule. With a background in school psychology, I knew schedules, structure and sleep were important for babies' behavior and development. But once I starting bringing babies home from the NICU, I knew a schedule would be necessary to keep some order in our chaotic world. And keep me sane! The feeding schedule was easy; I just continued the NICU feeding schedule as they came home, but the sleep schedule was another story.

I purchased "Healthy Sleep, Habits Happy Child" by Dr. Weissbluth to guide my babies' sleep training. However, between my limited free time and extreme sleep deprivation, reading an entire book was just not going to happen. So I did what I used to do in high school and college...I found the cliff notes...this quick reference guide from Christy! Complete lifesaver! The easy-to-read format allowed me to read the entire document in one sitting. I especially loved the personal tips and tricks Christy included. As a mother of three (including twins!), I trusted her advice and knew she had been just where I was at that time.

Once I began setting a sleep schedule in my household, I quickly learned it was not going to be easy. It took every ounce of willpower I had to implement the strategies consistently and effectively, but I did it. It took a couple of weeks to get settled in the routine of the schedule, and then we were able to work any kinks out. I kept Christy's notes close by to reference when I was questioning myself, or just needed a feeling of support. When I needed in-depth guidance or answers to detailed questions, my copy of "Healthy Sleep Habits,

Happy Child" really came in handy. It took a solid week of the cry-it-out method to get all six babies to sleep eight hours straight, but it was all worth it. A few months later they were able to drop the last dream feed. The transition to sleeping eleven to twelve hours was a breeze. Establishing a firm nap schedule took more time, but it happened.

To date, my kids are two-and-a-half years old and sleep a solid eleven hours at night and take a three-hour nap every afternoon. It isn't a fight to get them to bed and if they wake up early they are happy to entertain themselves in their room for a bit. I attribute my sleep training success to Christy's notes of Dr. Weissbluth's strategies. I specifically followed each strategy and every minute of hard work paid off in the long run. Trust me; it is worth your while. I recommend her notes to every single one of my friends with babies because it works! And, if it works with six babies at once, it can certainly work with one or two. You just have to hang in there and stick with it. You can do it!

So read the quick reference guide, use the strategies, and thank Christy later...after your eight hours of uninterrupted sleep.

# CHRISTY L. BRUNTON

## Lauren Perkins, mom to two-year-old sextuplets

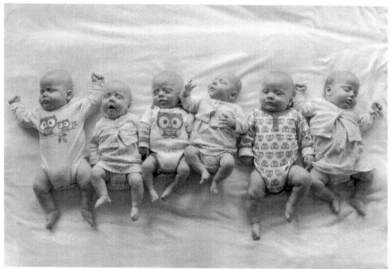

Photo credit: Allen Kramer, Texas Children's Hospital

# Introduction

A few notes about how this book is laid out before we jump in. This book is broken up by age and will contain the basic techniques taught by Dr. Weissbluth, but will also include my notes and specific actions I took to implement his techniques. I want to put a disclaimer here that all three of my children were pretty easy-going kids with no health issues, so if your child does have any health issues, I want you to consult a doctor before getting started. Also, Dr. Weissbluth discusses several sleep issues in-depth such as colic, snoring, night terrors and more in chapters four and ten of his book, as well as a few others. He goes into the theory behind these issues and how to get your child through them.

The beauty of this quick reference guide is because it is short you can read it all the way through one time to get the gist of his techniques then reference the sections you need often depending on the age of your child until you feel you have the techniques down. I have also created a Facebook page (search Sleep Training for the Exhausted Mom) to go along with this book where I will be checking in regularly to answer your sleep questions.

Let's get started.

# First six weeks

Remember, before you had kids when you used to say, "When I have my baby, we are going to just have him/her fit into OUR schedule." Okay, maybe it was just me or the friends I hung out with who thought life would not change much just because you add one little person to the family. Boy, were we wrong! Not only does your baby not just "fit into your schedule," but your baby BECOMES your schedule. Can I get an AMEN? Everything you do, every decision you make, revolves around whether this little human needs to eat or sleep or have a little tummy time. Spoiler alert...you will get your life back. I am here to tell you, it does get easier and being a mom is really so much fun and rewarding. I can only speak to where I am today, but when they are in school, although your schedule still revolves around your kids, there is much more time for doing what you want to do. I've digressed…

Back to you. Let's talk about those first six weeks. Don't worry, if it is your first baby you won't remember much about them. It is a mini war-zone and the memory of it will be a little foggy. In short, for the first six weeks, things are crazy. Don't worry too much about HOW you get through the first six weeks; the goal is just to get through them.

Focus on the eating schedule first and getting that straight and then it will be easier to work that feeding schedule into a consistent sleeping schedule. At this stage, especially for the first month, your baby will sleep A LOT, like literally most of the day. I know when it is your first baby it can be hard because you want them up and alert and maybe think they should be. But at this phase they need to sleep and you really should just take advantage of the time and sleep yourself. Reload and recharge!

Let me stop and add a little logistical note here. Throughout these notes, I will talk about my experiences with the twins (Taylor and Kennedy who are pictured on the cover), but also with my singleton (Reese). They were a little different since I exclusively breastfed my singleton (breastfeeding was much easier the second time around especially since it was just one) and with my twins I pumped and supplemented with formula. With the twins, since they were in the NICU, I was able to keep them on the NICU feeding schedule during the first six weeks. I still implemented the sleep training the same way for both the twins and my singleton, but altered them slightly to account for the challenge of twins. I try to denote "twin tips" throughout. These "twin tips" also work for triplets, quadruplets and beyond as seen with Lauren and her sextuplets.

During the first six weeks, here are some things I did to minimize the craziness.

- **Don't worry about a schedule at this point**: Feed them when they want to eat, let them sleep when they want to sleep. They will sleep a lot, like eighteen hours a day. At night, if you put your healthy one-week old down and they sleep a four-hour stretch, let them do so. They will wake up when they are hungry. You may be one of the lucky ones, but be prepared to be hated by your fellow new moms when you start telling your stories of your baby sleeping through the night at two weeks old. My advice changes if they are preemies. Consult your pediatrician, but I was told to keep waking them up to eat at least until they reach their original due date.

- **Eating schedule:** During the day, for the first six weeks, I woke them up every three hours to eat. From what I remember, it seems they started going four hours at night around seven weeks old, around five to six hours at two-and-a-half months (real age, not adjusted age), then at three-and-a-half months they were sleeping from 10 p.m. to 6 a.m. It was definitely a progression. For my singleton, I exclusively breastfed her and she did not follow this schedule. She was eating every two to three hours and didn't start sleeping longer stretches – even four hour stretches – until about four months old.

Note: Adjusted age, also called corrected age, is the age a preemie would be if they had been born on their due date. Adjusted ages are useful when evaluating a preemie's size and development.

- **Limit the amount of time you feed them:** With the twins I ran into the problem where I felt they took forever to eat and it was as if I was feeding them all the time. I remember it would take almost an hour-and-a-half for them to eat two ounces. It felt as soon as they were done eating they would sleep for an hour and it would be time to feed them again. I am sure this is not just a twin thing so this would apply to singletons too. When I told my pediatrician how long it took me to feed them, she told me I should let them eat for 30 minutes then stop. She said the extra milk I would try to get down them in the hour-and-a-half was not worth it. The calories they would get would not be much more. It worked and usually by the next feeding they were ready for a full feeding again.

- **If you are breastfeeding, the first six weeks are really tough:** It does get easier around six weeks, so hang in there. I breastfed my singleton and wanted to quit every week, but once I made it to six weeks, things got much easier. I know this is not the case for everyone and for some moms breastfeeding comes super easy (a topic for another book I guess).

- **Twin tip: Feed them at the same time/wake the other to eat:** The NICU got my girls on an every three hour feeding schedule which I tried to stick to. I would always feed them at the same time and always put them down to sleep together. And, I would always wake the second sleeping baby to eat. If you don't do this, you will go crazy because they will be on separate schedules and you will have no time for yourself. Sometimes at naps, once the first one woke up, I would feed her by herself to give her special bonding time with mommy and then once she was done I would wake the second one up and do the same. This still keeps them on schedule because they usually wake within 15 minutes of each other.

# Getting started with sleep training

Now that we have discussed the first six weeks, let's talk about the real reason you are reading this handy quick reference guide.

Sleeping! For the first year, you will have MANY questions on this topic. Next to my husband, Dr. Weissbluth was my second favorite person in the world (my hero really) who got me through my babies' first years. His book is very helpful and the theory behind why his method works really made sense to me. As I said before, I will do my best to hit the highlights in the next few pages, but for a more in-depth understanding you should have the book on your nightstand and read it when you have extra time. Dr. Weissbluth also has a version for multiples that is a good read if you have twins or more.

When I was pregnant there was a lot of hype around the "On Becoming Baby Wise" book. So, in the first month after the babies arrived, I read Baby Wise. But, after I was told about "Healthy Sleep Habits, Happy Child," I read it too and everything made much more sense to me. What you have probably heard about Baby Wise is it teaches the three-hour cycle of eat, play, and sleep (in that order). I am not saying it wasn't helpful…there was some good information in there. While I liked how it taught me how the schedule works, I felt I wasn't getting enough information on how to make the sleep part of the schedule work. This is what led me to Dr. Weissbluth's book.

What I like about his book is that it focuses on the sleep part of the equation and the importance of sleep which is really the area I had most of my questions. I was amazed when I found out newborns needed up to eighteen hours of sleep each day, babies up to one year need between fourteen and fifteen hours and toddlers need between twelve and fifteen hours. I think most books adopt the "eat, play and sleep" schedule, but forget to tell you how to get the sleep part right, which is what Dr. Weissbluth focuses on in his book. He also addresses sleep problems, growth spurts, the cry it out (CIO) method, etc. If I just scared you with the CIO talk, don't worry, we will get to that in due time. Just stay with me. It will be worth it.

# Six weeks to three months

You made it past the first six weeks and are now ready to get moving on sleep training. In this chapter you will find lots of my personal notes as I tried to implement what I read from Dr. Weissbluth. I will tell you, I consulted his book multiple times a day to make sure I was doing everything correctly. I even turned to some online chat rooms dedicated to sleep training so please visit my Facebook page if you have questions.

There is a lot here to take in but just take it step-by-step. At six weeks old, I officially started sleep training. I started slowly to get everyone used to it…including myself. Below are a few things I started implementing to get us going.

- **Move them out of your room:** At six-weeks old real age (not corrected), I started doing some things differently. With my twins, I moved them from my room into their own room, but still in the same crib. This helped me get more sleep because I wasn't waking up with every little sound I heard. Also, I really tried not to rush in when I heard them make a noise. I found if I would leave them for a minute, they would often fall back to sleep on their own.

- **The six week peak:** According to Dr. Weissbluth, all babies are most fussy, cry the most and are most wakeful at six weeks of age. I remember this being a really hard phase, especially at night. The swing became a true friend to me during this time. Around 7 p.m. each night, they sometimes would be so fussy I would turn to the swing to just get a few minutes of peace and quiet. This phase passes, I promise!

- **Bedtime routine:** Up until now, I didn't really have a solid routine at night. At six weeks, I started a bedtime routine which consisted of feeding them half their bottle, a bath (every other night), lotion and massage, pajamas, other half of the bottle, then to bed. I always put a classical music CD on (Baby Einstein) to soothe them to sleep, which I did until they were two years old.

- **Make as little noise as possible in the middle of the night:** My advice is to keep it dark, DO NOT change their diapers unless it is a blowout and put them straight back to bed after they eat. I found those diapers can hold a lot of pee and it woke them up when I would change them. For my twins, I would feed them at the same time in their boppies (one in each boppy on the floor).

If you are drifting off at this point, I need you to go grab some coffee because this is the crux of the book. Welcome to sleep training 101!

**What is sleeping training?:** With sleep training it's all about the two-hour wake rule. What I figured out from the book is sleep training is based on timing and watching your baby's sleep cues so you can catch them before they become overtired. This usually happens within two hours after they wake up or if it is first thing in the morning one-and-a-half hours after they wake. During these first weeks of sleep training, you are trying to understand your baby in order to figure out their best schedule. Watch for sleepy cues such as rubbing their eyes, your baby being less engaged with you, less vocal or starting to yawn. At this point, start your soothing-to-sleep routine. Soothing to sleep for us included me laying my girls on their tummies and rubbing their back. I would turn them over once they were good and asleep. Sometimes if they still weren't falling asleep, I would try the swing or bouncy chair. The goal at this point is to ESTABLISH the two-hour schedule…not to worry about HOW you are getting them to sleep. Even if they have to sleep on you during the first few days of the training, this could work too as long as you aren't making this the norm. The end-state is to get them on a solid sleeping schedule so you can put them in their crib and get some sleep yourself!

According to Dr. Weissbluth, sleep training begins with developing a sense of timing so you are trying to soothe your baby at the time when your baby is naturally getting drowsy before falling asleep. I found he was so right. If I would miss this window, I would have a screaming baby who would be overtired. Once they hit the overtired phase, it would be much harder for me to soothe them to sleep.

I officially started sleep training at six weeks of age. I admit six-weeks old is a tough age to start because at six-weeks old babies are at their peak of being fussy, fussy, fussy. All of mine were, that's for sure! But, I still think it is super-important to get going on the training because if you do, your baby will get it all figured out much quicker.

As I mentioned earlier, with Dr. Weissbluth's method, I had the girls sleeping through the night at three-and-a-half months (real age, this would be two-and-a-half months corrected age for them since they were one month early). I really worked to get them on a good nap schedule too.

Here is how it worked:

- I would put them down for their first nap **one to one-and-a-half hours** after they woke up for the day. To spell this out, if they wake up at 6:30 a.m., their first "nap" would be at 7:30 or 8 a.m. You can always look for sleep cues within the two-hour wake time, because sometimes they may only make it an hour-and-a-half. This was usually the case for mine when I first started sleep training. Especially in the morning, they would only make it an hour-and-a-half.

- Once they woke from the first nap, I would feed them first and then have playtime. This was the eat and play routine I learned from Baby Wise. But, when the two-hour mark would come around again, it was time to put them down for their next nap. So, if they were up from their first nap at 10:30 a.m., I would put them back down for their next nap at 12:30 p.m. or a little earlier if they were showing sleepy cues. Even if they seemed wide awake, I would still go put them down at the two-hour mark. And, I never put them down with a bottle or by nursing them. I only did this at nighttime. I distinctly remember my aunt telling me after weeks into the sleep training, "I am amazed at how easy they go to sleep for you. They seem wide awake but then they just go straight to sleep and even without a bottle."

- And then, follow the two-hour wake rule for the rest of the day. It works out to about four naps with bedtime around 9 p.m. or so (at three months old). **Most people try to keep their babies up too long during the day thinking it will tire them out, but really, babies can't be up for more than two hours without getting tired. I found this to be so true.**

- The goal is to get each of these naps to a couple of hours each or at least an hour-and-a-half around this age. If mine would wake up at the one-hour mark, I would sometimes let them cry for just a couple of minutes to see if they would go back to sleep. Many times this worked and they would sleep another 30 minutes to an hour. My point, don't go in at the first sound. Give them a chance to work it out on their own and fall back to sleep.

- o Example schedule:
    - 6:30 a.m. – Wake up for the day, bottle, tummy time
    - 8 a.m. – First nap. Let's say they only sleep for an hour and are up at 9 a.m., the next nap would be two hours from the wakeup time.
    - 11 a.m. – Try for the next nap. If they sleep until 12:30 p.m., get them up, feed them, play and try for their next nap two hours later.
    - 2:30 p.m. – Try for the next nap. If they sleep until 4:30 p.m. then I would try for a little cat nap at 6:30 or 7 p.m.
    - 7 p.m. – Try for a short nap.
    - 9 p.m. – Start bedtime routine.

- **But, what if they don't fall asleep when I put them down for their nap?:** Even if they didn't fall asleep, I would still put them down and give them the chance to try to fall asleep (usually ten to fifteen minutes). This helped them get used to their routine. If they did not fall asleep, no big deal, I waited two more hours and tried again or I would look for their sleepy cues and try again then. The trick is to catch them before they get overtired. You do this by watching for their sleepy cues.

- **Don't expect too much:** From six weeks to three months old, don't expect them to magically understand how naps work. The "morning nap" will not truly develop until four months old. It was actually kind of weird to watch how this nap magically started working at almost four months exactly. The goal right now is to make sure you are following the two-hour wake rule and you are teaching them how to sleep in their cribs and how to soothe themselves to sleep. As adults, we already know how to soothe ourselves back to sleep if we wake up in the middle of the night. We learned it somewhere, somehow. So, how do we teach our children this important skill? Sleep training! It is our job to teach our children how to get themselves back to sleep on their own. It is a skill they will use their entire lives.

- **Pacifiers or soothers are okay:** All three of mine used pacifiers to soothe themselves. My youngest switched to her thumb around four months, a habit we broke at four years old. The twins used a pacifier for about six months and then dropped it on their own. A lot of times I would put them down on their stomach with a pacifier to get them to sleep, pat their backs a little bit and when they were asleep I would go in and turn them over. Because I was still very nervous about Sudden Infant Death Syndrome (SIDS) I only did this when nothing else worked and made sure to check on them every few minutes until I could turn them back to their backs. Once they could lift their heads when they were older, I didn't worry about SIDS as much anymore. It's okay to put your baby in bed during the drowsy-but-awake state.

- **Other soothing techniques:** Dr. Weissbluth suggests reducing stimulation, light, noise and activity. You can soothe your baby to sleep by swaddling, nursing, rocking, singing, massage or anything that might otherwise calm your baby. Most babies need only one of these, and too many at once may be over-stimulating. However, a colicky baby may require longer effort and more techniques. If your zero to four-month old baby continues crying, don't ignore the cries. Continue soothing him, but if he falls asleep during the soothing, **do not wake them** before placing them in the crib. (Dr. Weissbluth seems particularly irritated by books that suggest otherwise).

- **Motion sleep:** Early on in the first months, I would not worry too much about having them sleep in the swing. It is more important to get them used to sleeping at certain times and if it is in a swing or on your chest, this is okay. However, when they reach three to four months, you don't want to promote sleep aids; you want them to fall asleep and stay asleep on their own. According to Dr. Weissbluth, motion sleep is not very restful sleep and they end up waking up more tired. I tried to stop any motion sleep by four months old, but every so often I would let them fall asleep in their swings if I was having trouble getting them down. Then, once they fell asleep, I would turn the swing off to make it still.

- **Try to be at home:** If you are going to do this, you need to be "all-in." The best way to approach this is to be at your house so your baby can sleep in their own crib. If you try this while driving around or doing a nap in the stroller, it will not be as productive.

- **Night sleep:** It is around this time, or closer to seven or eight weeks, when your baby will start sleeping longer stretches at night. I recommend you let them go as long as they can at night and not try to wake them for a feeding unless they need it.

- **If all else fails:** If they just wouldn't go to sleep, I would let them play, feed them at their next feeding time and usually they would start getting fussy and showing sleepy cues, so I would put them down again. If they slept for only 30 minutes, then I would plan on trying to put them down two hours from when they woke up. I had to be pretty flexible. And, at this age, mine were on a different schedule every day since each day started at a different time depending on when they woke up at night to eat. They didn't really start getting on a consistent schedule until they slept through the night and then at that time I was able to establish a wake-up time. Around six months old, I was able to plan around their schedule because it was the same every day. This was a beautiful time! I could actually get things done again.

- **If your baby has colic:** Dr. Weissbluth spends a lot of time on this topic in his book and gives some great tips on getting through this and the theory behind why this happens. He sums it up by saying most of the sleep issues associated with colicky babies disappear by four months of age.

- **Special events or vacations:** I realize there will be some days you have special events or go on a vacation or weekend getaways and can't stick to the schedule. I tried to do the best I could when we were away. I would try to follow our schedule as much as possible knowing there would be times we couldn't get all the naps in. The benefit to having your babies on a sleep schedule is when you do return home it only takes them a couple of days to get back on the schedule and maybe only one night of using the cry-it-out method (I will address this a little later).

- **Twin tip - separate them if you are having problems:** If you are having trouble getting your multiples to sleep and are not sure who the problem is, you may try separating them for a week or two so you can learn the sleep patterns of both of your babies. Once you have figured their patterns out, you can move them back to the same room. I ended up having to keep mine separated for naps starting at nine months old. When they were together during the day, they just wouldn't go to sleep. I did keep them in the same room at night which didn't seem to bother them.

By now I hope you feel you have a good, clear explanation on the basics of the technique. If you are consistent, I promise it will pay off. I can't tell you how many moms have called me after a couple weeks of trying this to say how much better they feel after implementing a good schedule. You have time for yourself, you have time for your spouse and you have a happy and well-rested baby or babies in my case. There are a few other things worth mentioning at this point that are important parts of sleep training.

- Getting your baby on a good day schedule will ultimately affect them sleeping at night. Dr. Weissbluth says sleeping well during the day will improve night sleeping and conversely, nap deprivation causes night waking.

- If you are working parents it will be tough to want to stick to this because you will feel like you aren't getting to see your baby much. As a working mom myself, I too felt very guilty about this. What made me feel better was the fact I knew I was doing what was best for my children. I got so many compliments on how well-behaved and easy-going my children were as babies and I attributed it to their sleep schedule. Even now, at six and nine years old, my kids are focused and well-adjusted which I think has a lot to do with the fact I trained them to be good sleepers.

- Dr. Weissbluth shares many stories of other moms' struggles in the book. It is worth reading them. One of the mom's is quoted saying, "Babies yearn for routines and respond unbelievably to them. Again, we feel we have two of the happiest, sweetest children, and knowing that teaching them good sleep habits, and, more importantly, the ability to fall asleep unassisted is the best gift you can ever give!"

- If your child has a childcare provider during the day I would recommend you give the sleep schedule to them and ask them to follow it. I was very clear with my childcare provider that she had to use the schedule. After a week of using it, she liked it so much she got the other three kids she watched on the same schedule! I never did receive thank you notes from those parents…oh well.

- I know this tip won't work for everyone, but when I first started sleep training I took a Thursday and Friday off of work so I could have four full days to focus on getting the sleep training in place. I did the same thing when we were transitioning to a new part of training such as dropping the morning nap. I found when I led the sleep training it worked much better than trying to get my childcare provider to focus on it.

# Four to six months

Four months was really the time where it seemed all of the hard work I put into sleep training during those first few months started to pay off! Because I started "practicing" early and stayed consistent with the routine (even if it didn't work every time) I could tell at four months old, things just started to click. For us, the morning nap started to happen pretty regularly and the night sleep became much easier.

To start this section off, I took some tips directly from Dr. Weissbluth (including page numbers from his book) with some of my personal notes included after.

- **Starting the day:** Most children will awake to start the day around 7 a.m., but there is a wide range between 6-8 a.m. (p. 246)

- **First nap:** The first nap occurs around 9 a.m. and it may last about an hour or two. Sometimes, you will stretch your child to get to this time, or you may wake your child up at 7 a.m. in order for them to be able to take this nap. Remember, previously you focused on maintaining short intervals of wakefulness, but now you try to anticipate your child's predictable best nap time. If your child takes this nap too early or too late, then it is difficult for them to take the second nap on time. This morning nap disappears between fifteen and twenty-one months of age. (p. 248)

- **Second nap:** The second nap occurs around 1 p.m. and may last about an hour or two. The most common problem at this nap time is too long of an interval of wakefulness following the first nap. This can cause your child to become overtired. The time window for this second nap is between 12 and 2 p.m., but you may notice your child's own time window during which it is easiest to fall asleep is much narrower. This afternoon nap commonly continues for about four years. (p. 257)

- **Third nap:** The third nap may or may not occur. If it does, it may happen between 3 and 5 p.m. Also, the duration of this nap may vary, but it is usually a very brief nap. This nap tends to disappear by about eight months. (p. 258)

- **Bedtime:** Because of the variability of the third nap, the bedtime may also differ. Most children are asleep between 7 and 9 p.m. The most common problem at bedtime is keeping your child up too late. If the child is put to sleep after their time of tiredness, they have more difficulty falling asleep and staying asleep. If you keep your child up past the time when they are drowsy – for example, because you return home late from work – then you are depriving your child of sleep. Please try to avoid making your child overtired just to meet your schedule. (p. 259)

**My notes:**

- **Morning nap starts to develop:** Around this age, you will notice the morning nap will start to lengthen. I was amazed with Reese how I would put her down for a nap around 9 a.m., which was about two hours (sometimes an hour-and-a-half) after she woke up (if she woke at 7 a.m.) and she would sleep for almost two hours. Sometimes she would get tired a little earlier, so I would put her down earlier as well, but she would still sleep the two hours.

- **Establish a wake-up time:** Since the twins were sleeping through the night at this point, I tried to establish a wake-up time of 7 a.m. If they woke up earlier, I did my best not to go to them before 7 a.m. or I would go in and try to soothe them back to sleep. At 7 a.m., I would walk in, open the blinds and make it very clear this was wake-up time. By starting the day at the same time every day, we now had a consistent routine I could count on.

- Our schedule at this point was:
    - 7 a.m. – wake up for the day, bottle, tummy time
    - 9 a.m. – morning nap
    - 1 p.m. – afternoon nap
    - 4 p.m. – sometimes short cat nap
    - 7 p.m. – start bedtime routine
    - 10 p.m. – dream feed

- **Afternoon sleep was still a mess:** I still tried to put them back down for an afternoon nap, but they would usually only sleep for an hour or so. This meant I typically would have a third cat nap between 4 and 5 p.m.

- **For naps, watch the clock and wait ten minutes to go in:** The goal of this exercise is to teach them how to soothe themselves back to sleep. For naptime, put them in their crib. Even if they didn't fall asleep, I would always lay mine down at the scheduled nap time and give them at least thirty minutes in their cribs. If they start crying, let them cry for ten minutes. I would literally look at a clock to see when ten minutes was up and 95% of the time they would be asleep well before then. Ten minutes can feel like a long time when babies are crying so just watch the clock and try not to let yourself go into the room before the ten minutes is up. Sometimes it may take you stepping outside or doing a quick chore to get your mind off of it or maybe checking in on the latest episode of Ellen (my go-to show during maternity leave).

- **If it's not working:** If they are still crying, go into the room, give them their blanket or soother and then leave. Let them cry for ten more minutes. Go in again and maybe try putting them on their stomach and patting their back (I would turn mine back over onto their back when they were sleeping as I was nervous about SIDS at this point still). If nothing works, then go ahead and get them up and try again a couple of hours later. I would sometimes try the swing as well. Motion sleep is not restful sleep, so try not to let this become a habit.

  o Dr. Weissbluth says if the nap is substantially less than thirty minutes you should try to leave your baby alone for an additional thirty to sixty minutes, even if they cry, to see if they will fall asleep on their own. If the nap is substantially longer than thirty minutes, it is less likely they will return to sleep so you can either leave your baby alone for another thirty minutes or go to your baby immediately and not let them cry anymore. (p. 249)

- **Get rid of the evening cat nap and make that bedtime**: At four months old, I also got rid of the last nap and made that bedtime. My goal was to feed them right before bed (around 7 or 8 p.m.). At this age, the twins started sleeping through the 12:30 a.m. feeding and then eventually through the 3:30 a.m. feeding as well. Reese, who was breastfed, ate again at 10 p.m. and then at 3 a.m. up until she was six months old.

- **Bedtime around 7 or 8 p.m.:** I started the bedtime routine two hours after their final afternoon nap, which was around 7 or 8 p.m. This is the only part of the day when I would give a bottle right before bed. With Reese, I nursed her right before bed.

- **Dream feed:** With the twins and with Reese, I still did a dream feed at four months old. I would wake them around 10 p.m. and give them a bottle (nursed Reese). The twins were sleeping through the night at this stage (they started sleeping through the night at three-and-a-half months due to the sleep training we started at six weeks old). Reese still wasn't. Reese was exclusively breastfed until six months old and still got up once a night (around 3 a.m.). At six months old, she would sleep from 10 p.m. to 7 a.m. I did have to let Reese CIO starting at six months old to get her to drop the 3 a.m. feed. It took about three nights.

- **CIO method:** If they were having trouble falling asleep at bedtime, I would do the same thing as I did for naps. I would wait ten minutes before going in and then try and soothe them. If it still didn't work, this is when I would start the CIO method. This method was the magic bullet to finally get everyone to sleep through the night and four months old is the age I recommend trying it. With Reese, since she was breastfed, I waited to push her to sleep through the night until six months old. With the twins I tried the CIO method at four months old and it took three nights to get them to sleep through the night from 10 p.m. (after their dream feed) to 7 a.m. There are several CIO methods, which I will explain in the next section.

# Cry-it-out

Yes, I just said cry-it-out, so please don't freak out if this method is not for you. I put this in the "four to six month old" section because doctors feel this is the safest time to start the method. Before four months there may be psychological or physical reasons your baby is crying so you don't want to ignore those. Sleep training is still effective without CIO, but may take a little longer.

Why don't we start with the story of two moms I met at work. I won't say their names, but both were on their first babies and it was apparent each of them was having sleep struggles in their households. I met each of them around the point when their babies were four months old and they were struggling with getting them to sleep through the night and also with their nap schedules being off. I, of course, offered them my quick reference guide but decided to give them a pep-talk as well. Since their babies were four-months old, I really encouraged them to try CIO. Right away, I knew this would be a hard sell as they didn't seem too excited about the method. I tried to explain that you are actually doing your baby a favor. You are teaching them how to get themselves back to sleep on their own. I explained this is very similar to what you and I do each night. We wake up multiple times a night but we already know how to get ourselves back to sleep. Babies don't and you have to teach them. If you run to them every time they cry and don't let them try to figure it out, they will never learn how to soothe themselves.

I guess when I put it that way they somehow talked themselves into giving it a shot. I told them it will take at least three nights and not to give up before then. I also told them all three of mine started out crying for more than an hour straight the first night but by night three they were down to five minutes and then on the fourth night it was zero crying! The next morning you could tell they tried the method and had a similar experience with the long bouts of crying and told me they even shed several tears themselves. But, what I loved is on day four they both came back in and said, "You will never believe it, but they are sleeping through the night and I can't believe it worked." I remember smiling and then leading them to Dr. Weissbluth's full book so they could implement the rest of his methods for day sleep.

If I have convinced you this might work, keep reading. If not, feel free to skip forward to the next section. Sleep training still works without the CIO method, it just may take longer to get your baby to sleep through the night and you yourself will be losing several hours and days of precious sleep.

Here's how it works (p. 210-215):

- Ignoring, extinction – According to Dr. Weissbluth, the idea is to respond if you think your child is hungry but not at other times. My interpretation of this method (and this is the method I used) is to ignore them. It is one of the hardest things you will do during your first year of parenting. You pick a night to start and then once you have put your child to bed and checked the surroundings are safe, they are fed, changed and comfortable, the moment you hear the first bout of crying, you just ignore them! It may mean you are sitting outside the room listening in and possibly crying yourself, but you DON'T GO IN. It will seem like an eternity but they do stop crying and they do fall asleep and most are happy as a clam when you wake them in the morning. Even though there may be lots of intense crying up front, this method actually has the least amount of overall crying because the problem is fixed by day two or three. It also allows you to be more consistent than some of the methods below. It works quickly so there is a smaller likelihood you will give up.

If the extinction method is not for you, you can try the other methods below. Beware, these take longer than the extinction method but still can get you the results you need. The key to these methods is to not give up and to remain consistent. This is where most parents go wrong and why these are harder to implement.

- Controlled crying, partial ignoring, graduated extinction – According to Dr. Weissbluth, this is a variation of extinction. Leave your baby for about five minutes, then return and soothe him back to the sleepy state. If loud crying recurs, leave your baby for ten minutes and then repeat the soothing process. The sequence repeats with an additional five minutes of ignoring the crying until they fall asleep. Another method is to also increase the time of ignoring, but increase the time by about five minutes every two days. This may work but could take four to nine nights. The controlled crying method may appear less harsh than "extinction" and works well with many children.

- Check and console – You quietly enter whenever your baby cries to see if they are all right and gently soothe them in the darkness, but try not to pick them up. Leave after they are soothed and then return if they start crying again. You keep doing this until they fall back asleep.

- Scheduled awakenings – Parents note the approximate times when their child wakes up at night and the parents wake their child before those times. The child is changed, if needed, and soothed back to sleep. Dr. Weissbluth says research has shown extinction works much faster than scheduled awakenings, but scheduled awakenings do work. (p. 297)

For me personally, I chose the extinction method which was incredibly hard! I specifically remember Reese's story. At six months old with Reese, she cried for one-hour-and-forty minutes the first night, one-hour-and-thirty minutes the second night, forty-five minutes the third night and then she slept through the night on the fourth night. I felt like a horrible mother at first and it was hard to get my husband on board with everything too. Both of us wanted to go in every few minutes. And, I would be lying if I didn't tell you I might have army-crawled into the room a couple of times making sure she couldn't see me to check on her. I remember having to talk myself out of the fact that something was wrong in there. What if she is sick, what if she got her finger caught in something, what if her diaper is hurting her? I had every excuse possible going through my head on why I should give up on CIO. What fixed everything is when I would go to wake her up in the morning, she would be smiling at me which made me feel so much better. Her big grin proved to me the CIO method was not as harsh as I originally thought. There was obviously no harm done.

I also loved what this one mom said from Dr. Weissbluth's book (p. 297). She said, "I kept thinking it must be horribly frightening for a baby, who is unable to communicate except through crying, to be left alone in a room to cry. What helped convince me, however, (in addition to utter and complete exhaustion), was the realization that as long as I stayed in Lauren's room she screamed anyway. Walking, rocking, singing – none of these quieted her anymore. The only thing that calmed her was endless, nonstop nursing! I finally came to the conclusion that as long as Lauren was going to be miserable crying anyway, she might as well be learning something positive from it – learning to go to sleep."

# SLEEP TRAINING FOR THE EXHAUSTED MOM

# Six to nine months

At this point, you should feel like a pro when it comes to sleep training, or you should at least have the basics down. The good news is even if you haven't started sleep training yet and are picking up this quick reference guide for the first time now, it is never too late to start implementing the method. You will just need to jump back up to the top to get the basics. Around six months old, a few new things will start to happen with your baby and their sleep training journey.

- **Afternoon nap starts to develop:** Around this age, you will notice the afternoon nap will start to form. Like the morning nap that to me just magically started working at four months, I felt the same about the afternoon nap at six months. This nap usually starts between 1 and 2 p.m. and lasts until 3 or 4 p.m. (depending on how the morning nap went).

- **For breastfed babies, the middle of night feeding *may* go away:** For my third baby, Reese, I moved her to formula starting at seven months. At my six month appointment, the pediatrician told me she really didn't need the 3 a.m. feeding anymore and was just waking up for habit.

- **Dropped the dream feed:** With the twins, I tried dropping the 10 p.m. dream feed. They were starting to get solids in the daytime so I decided to try to make 7 p.m. their bedtime with no dream feed. I had to use the CIO method, but it worked within a few days.

- **Some babies may need to be fed in the middle of the night:** When rereading Dr. Weissbluth's book to get ready to publish my quick reference guide, I was surprised when he mentioned some babies may start waking back up in the middle of the night for a feeding. It makes sense though. He says because you are now putting your baby to sleep for the night at 7 p.m. they may actually be hungry at 2 or 3 a.m. I didn't have this issue with my girls, but if your baby starts waking up, you may want to try feeding them and then once you think they are through this stage try CIO again if needed.

- **Teething may cause issues:** Reese began teething at eight months old and started waking up again the middle of the night. She was not taking much of her bottle during the day since her gums hurt her, so she would wake up at night to eat. I went ahead and fed her since I knew she was hungry and didn't try to get her sleeping through the night again until the tooth broke through. With my twins, teething did not affect them as much and didn't seem to affect their sleeping.

- **Formula babies sleeping 12 hours:** At six months old, my twins were sleeping 7 p.m. to 7 a.m. pretty consistently.

- **My exclusively breastfed baby dropped the 10 p.m. feed around nine months old:** Up until eight months of age, I still would wake Reese up to feed her at 10 p.m. At nine months old, I decided to try and drop that feeding. After a couple of nights, it worked and she started sleeping from 7 p.m. to 7 a.m.

# One year to four years old

Hopefully, by this point you are patting yourself on the back! You did it. You made it through your first year and your baby is sleeping! You are sleeping yourself and everyone in the family is happy, happy, happy.

- **At one year, the first nap will start to go away:** My girls dropped their first nap around fifteen months and just went to one nap from about 1 to 4 p.m. This was definitely a progression. Around one year, they took the first nap sometimes, but by fifteen months, it was gone completely.

- **Between three and four years old, afternoon nap goes away:** At four years old, all three of my girls were still taking a nap from 2 to 4 p.m. on most days. Some days we had no nap at all and that was okay.

- **Missing naps:** I did notice missing a nap here and there at one to two years old was not that big of a deal. BUT, if they went too many days without a nap it definitely caught up with them and they were overtired. At three or four years old we took naps when we could, but it wasn't mandatory anymore.

- **This was interesting…:** Dr. Weissbluth states by three years of age, children who do not nap or who nap very little are often described as non-adaptable or even hyperactive. Adaptability is thought to be a very important trait for school success. Why this point was so interesting to me is because you hear so much these days about attention deficit hyperactivity disorder. It makes me wonder (Dr. Weissbluth doesn't say this), if a child's hyperactivity is really just a state of exhaustion and they are running off of adrenalin.

I am not a doctor but this seems suspicious to me.

- **Sick or overtired?:** When I reread Dr. Weissbluth's book recently I read a point that made me think of all the times my child was complaining of a tummy ache or headache but seemed to be fine. No fever, no vomiting. He states, if your child doesn't appear to be very sick but has frequent headaches or episodes of vague abdominal pain, especially near the end of the day, ask yourself if they might be over overtired? Looking back on my three girls and their tummy ache complaints, this point really made me think that maybe they were just tired.

# Troubleshooting

I know I make this sound so easy, but I can promise with my first two it wasn't easy at first. Here are a few tips to help you if you are having trouble.

- Stay consistent. If the naps just aren't working, just stick to the schedule. Keep focusing on the two hour wake rule and watch for the sleepy cues. Be patient, especially if you are trying a new technique. Give it a few days to work.

- If you miss the sleepy cues and your baby is overtired, focus on soothing techniques such as swaddling, rocking, swinging, etc. Then try the nap again as soon as you can calm them down.

- If you are having trouble with an early wake-up time, consult Dr. Weissbluth's book. He spends a lot of time talking about moving the bedtime earlier to help with the wake-up time. I know this sounds counterintuitive, but he believes sleep begets sleep.

- If you are having a bad day with sleep training, take a break! Wake up and try again tomorrow. Missing one day of training won't affect your baby.

- If you are a working mom, you may need to take a few vacation days to work with your baby yourself to instill the sleep training techniques and make sure they are being done correctly. This extra, focused time will pay off.

- One thing I tried when I was having trouble figuring out a good schedule for my twins was a sleep log. I've included an example below. The first chart is twin-specific since it has Baby A and Baby B written vertically in each column (I only included Sunday – Tuesday). The second one is for a singleton. I had a color-coded system so I could watch patterns to see if there were natural rhythms my babies were falling into when it came to a nap schedule. It was very helpful to see it plotted in color on a chart.

Each square denotes a different color so you can tell the patterns. I did "red" for asleep, "blue" for eat, "green" for playtime and "yellow" for down for nap, but awake in bed. Seeing the colors on the chart helped me identify patterns easily.

Full downloadable versions will be available on my Facebook page.

| Time | Sun | Sun | Mon | Mon | Tues | Tues |
|---|---|---|---|---|---|---|
| 5:00 am | | | | | | |
| 4:00 am | | | | | | |
| 3:00 am | | | | | | |
| 2:00 am | B | B | B | B | B | B |
| 1:00 am | | | | | | |
| 12:00 pm | A | A | A | A | A | A |
| 11:00 pm | | | | | | |
| 10:00 pm | B | B | B | B | B | B |
| 9:00 pm | | | | | | |
| 8:00 pm | Y | Y | Y | Y | Y | Y |
| 7:00 pm | | | | | | |
| 6:00 pm | | | | | | |
| 5:00 pm | A | B | A | B | A | B |
| 4:00 pm | | | | | | |
| 3:00 pm | | | | | | |
| 2:00 pm | | | | | | |
| 1:00 pm | | | | | | |
| 12:00 pm | | | | | | |
| 11:00 am | | | | | | |
| 10:00 am | | | | | | |
| 9:00 am | | | | | | |
| 8:00 am | | | | | | |
| 7:00 am | | | | | | |
| 6:00 am | | | | | | |

Asleep

Eat

Playtime

Down for nap, but awake in bed

~66~

# SLEEP TRAINING FOR THE EXHAUSTED MOM

| Time | Sun | Mon | Tues | Wed | Thurs | Fri | Sat |
|------|-----|-----|------|-----|-------|-----|-----|
| 5:00 am | | | | | | | |
| 4:00 am | | | | | | | |
| 3:00 am | | | | | | | |
| 2:00 am | | | | | | | |
| 1:00 am | | | | | | | |
| 12:00 pm | | | | | | | |
| 11:00 pm | | | | | | | |
| 10:00 pm | | | | | | | |
| 9:00 pm | | | | | | | |
| 8:00 pm | | | | | | | |
| 7:00 pm | | | | | | | |
| 6:00 pm | | | | | | | |
| 5:00 pm | | | | | | | |
| 4:00 pm | | | | | | | |
| 3:00 pm | | | | | | | |
| 2:00 pm | | | | | | | |
| 1:00 pm | | | | | | | |
| 12:00 pm | | | | | | | |
| 11:00 am | | | | | | | |
| 10:00 am | | | | | | | |
| 9:00 am | | | | | | | |
| 8:00 am | | | | | | | |
| 7:00 am | | | | | | | |
| 6:00 am | | | | | | | |

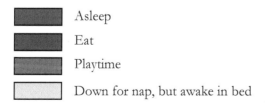

Asleep

Eat

Playtime

Down for nap, but awake in bed

# Final thoughts

Start sleep training early and be consistent. It may start with a lot of crying at first, but will prevent a lot of crying in the long run. Also, you have to be patient. With all training in life, you have to teach and then reteach and then practice. Your child won't get it on the first day. You have to keep at it to see the best results.

One thing I loved in Dr. Weissbluth's book was all of the studies he quoted. To be honest, as a first-time and exhausted mom I read right over these. All I wanted was to get to the heart of the techniques so I skimmed the theory. But, when I read his book again to get ready to publish this quick reference guide, I read it with a whole new view. I read it as a parent of older kids and found some of the theory to be fascinating. A few of the highlights taken from chapter two are below but there are several other interesting studies throughout the book you should check out.

- Several studies showed how naps are important for learning and cognitive development in children.

- Chronic sleepiness in infants and young children impair cognitive development but this will not become apparent until the child is much older and challenged by complex tasks.

- Three year olds who nap are more adaptable than those who did not. They were more fun to be around, more social and less demanding.

- In 1925, the father of the Stanford-Binet Intelligence Test, Dr. Lewis M. Tiernan, published his landmark book, Genetic Studies of Genius. He compared approximately 600 children with IQ scores over 140 to a group of almost 2,700 children with IQ scores below 140. For every age examined, the gifted children slept longer! Two years later, about 5,000 Japanese schoolchildren were studied and those with better grades slept longer as well!

- One study examined the effect of a single night of sleep restriction in children between 10 and 14 years old. The researchers noted there were impairments in verbal creativity, abstract thinking and concept formation and in complex problem solving.

My final thoughts on this subject are healthy sleep habits are not just about "how do I get my baby to sleep through the night?" I know this is the million-dollar question all new parents ask. I know I did. Healthy sleep habits are about the 24-hour sleep cycle and teaching techniques that will be with your children through adulthood. Day sleep is as important as night sleep and getting it right all starts with sleep training. Babies won't learn this or fall into the pattern by themselves (unless you are extremely lucky!). As a parent, it is our job to get them there; to teach them the technique, similar to how you would teach them to ride a bike or tie their shoes. It takes teaching and it takes practice. As a result, you will get a happy, well rested and adjusted child who likes knowing what comes next. I am still reaping the benefits of all the hard work I put in that first year with my two nine year olds and six year old. If I can do it with twins and a singleton, my friend Lauren can do it with sextuplets and hundreds of my friends from twins club who tested these notes can do it with their twins, you can too! So, go ahead and get started and if you run into any bumps in the road, head over to my Facebook page (search using the title of this book) to get answers to your real-time problems. I am sure other moms will have the same questions.

Good luck and happy sleeping!

# Quotes from other moms who found these notes helpful

"Routine, routine, routine is essential! Waking up the second twin because their sibling was waking up to eat was so important. At times I felt bad about waking up the sleeping baby, but eventually when they became synchronized with each other it was a life saver for all of us! And, I can't say enough about these nap tips and suggestions, because an overtired baby equals a fussy baby equals an overtired mommy." – *Sonia Cacique, mom to one-year-old boy/girl twins*

"I attribute my sleep training success to Christy's notes on Dr. Weissbluth's book. I specifically followed each strategy and every minute of hard work paid off in the long run. Trust me; it is worth your while. I recommend her notes to every single one of my friends with babies because it works! And if it works with six babies at once, it can certainly work for one or two. You just have to hang in there and stick with it. You can do it! So read the quick reference guide, use Dr. Weissbluth's strategies, and thank Christy later ... after your eight hours of uninterrupted sleep." – *Lauren Perkins, mom to two-year-old sextuplets*

# SLEEP TRAINING FOR THE EXHAUSTED MOM

"As Christy's sister-in-law I heard her going on and on about sleep training but wasn't so sure about the method when my first baby came along. At the time, I felt that my son would not respond well to sleep training. I just kept hoping it would happen naturally over time. Now, my son is 3 years old and still rarely sleeps through the night! With my second baby, who just turned six months old, I thought I would give it a try. I knew better than to hope it would just come naturally. I read Christy's notes in one night and was excited to get started immediately the next day. I am still only in the first week of training, but have been amazed that it is actually working. Within a few days, my little girl is putting herself down at the two-hour mark for her naps and has started sleeping through the night without waking up. I was afraid that at six months old I had started it too late, but Christy assured me that as long as I was consistent and stuck to Dr. Weissbluth's methods, it would eventually work. I am happy to report that we are at the 5 day mark and we are both making progress each day." – *Becca Brunton, mom to three-year-old boy and six-month-old girl*

"These notes really helped us get our little girl on a good schedule. The two-hour rule was a lifesaver. She wouldn't always want to nap but it gave us the next steps. Every book or article I had read before gave you an initial plan but not what to do when our little one didn't want to follow our tidy schedule. Now she sleeps ten to twelve hours a night and takes two naps a day. The best part is that when she deviates I am ready for what I will do next." — *Laura Aronson, mom to eight-month-old girl*

"I didn't do sleep training with my first two children, but with child number three I knew we needed a plan. The difference was like night and day. The scheduling really does work and it has been a much smoother experience following the sleep schedule and knowing what sleep cues to look for." — *Amy Krystof, mom to nine-year-old boy, seven-year-old girl and six-month-old girl*

# References

Weissbluth, Marc. *Healthy Sleep Habits, Happy Child: A Step-by-step Program for a Good Night's Sleep.* New York: Ballantine, 2005. Print.

Ezzo, Gary, and Robert Bucknam. *On Becoming Baby Wise: Giving Your Infant the Gift of Nighttime Sleep.* Louisiana, MO: Parent-Wise Solutions, 2006. Print.

Made in the USA
Charleston, SC
07 February 2015